A Pair of Pears

by Rebecca Felix

amicus readers

Ideas for Parents and Teachers

Amicus Readers let children practice reading informational texts at the earliest reading levels. Familiar words and concepts with close photo-text matches support early readers.

Before Reading
- Discuss the cover photo with the child. What does it tell him?
- Ask the child to predict what she will learn in the book.

Read the Book
- "Walk" through the book and look at the photos. Let the child ask questions.
- Read the book to the child, or have the child read independently.

After Reading
- Use the matching quiz at the end of the book to review the text.
- Prompt the child to make connections. Ask: *Can you think of other words that sound the same but have different meanings and spellings?*

Amicus Readers are published by Amicus
P.O. Box 1329, Mankato, MN 56002
www.amicuspublishing.us

Produced for Amicus by The Peterson Publishing Company and Red Line Editorial.

Editor Jenna Gleisner
Designer Jake Nordby
Printed in the United States of America
Mankato, MN
January, 2014
PA10001
10 9 8 7 6 5 4 3 2 1

Library of Congress Cataloging-in-Publication Data

Felix, Rebecca, 1984-
  A pair of pears / Rebecca Felix.
     pages cm. -- (Homophones)
  K to Grade 3.
  Audience: Age 6
  Includes bibliographical references and index.
  ISBN 978-1-60753-571-3 (hardcover : alk. paper) -- ISBN 978-1-60753-655-0 (pdf ebook)
  1. English language--Homonyms--Juvenile literature. I. Title.
PE1595.F45 2014
  428'.1--dc23
                            2013044010

Photo Credits: Tomo Jesenicnik/Shutterstock Images, cover, 1; Michel Borges/Shutterstock Images, 3; Shutterstock Images, 5, 9, 11, 13, 14–15, 16 (top left), 16 (top right), 16 (middle left), 16 (middle right), 16 (bottom left); Catalin Petolea/Shutterstock Images, 6; Julic Metkalova/Shutterstock Images, 10, 16 (bottom right)

Homophones are words that sound the same. But they have different meanings and spellings. What homophones can we find when we count?

3

pear
pair

A **pear** is a fruit. A **pair** is a group of two. We pick a **pair** of **pears**.

two
too

Eli picks **two** bunches of grapes. That is **too** many to eat at one time!

four
for

We split an orange into **four** slices. We will eat them **for** a snack.

9

eight
ate

Belle found **eight** strawberries. She **ate** two and gave away the rest!

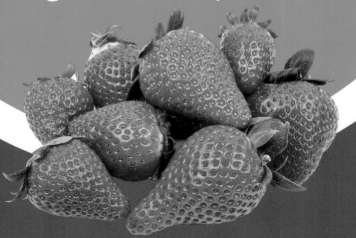

some sum

Eli eats **some** of his grapes. He counts the ones he has left. The **sum** is the total amount of grapes he has.

piece
peace

A **piece** of fruit is one bit or slice. Sharing is a great way to make **peace!**

Match each homophone to its picture!

pair

pear

ate

eight

peace

piece